# CLICK, POST, SUCCEED

## Social Media & Digital Marketing

# FOR KIDS



Nicolas Bahamon

**Published by QBO Publishing**
A division of QBO Corporation
8333 NW 53rd Street, Suite 450
Miami, Florida 33166

Library of Congress Cataloging-in-Publication Data
**Library of Congress Number:**
**Author:** Nicolas Bahamon
**Cover Art by:** Felipe Bahamon - Colombia
**Graphic Art Advisor:** David Herrera - Venezuela
**Edited by:** Alexander Estrada - Mexico
**Subjects: LCSH:** Social Media and Children. | Internet and Children. | Mass Media and Children Social Aspects.
Classification: LC Record available at



10 9 8 7 6 5 4 3 2 1

First Edition: December 2023

ISBN: 978-0-9961343-8-5 (Paperback)
ISBN: 978-0-9961343-7-8 (Hardback)
ISBN: 978-0-9961343-9-2 (eBook)
www.book.chainzd360.com



Printed in Unites States of America

To my Family!

# OPENING

My absolute favorite thing is soccer, and I practically lace up my shoes every single day. Rainy days are the pits, though, because that means no soccer for me. However, when I'm stuck indoors, I dive into some video games. It's fun, but it's just not the same as kicking the ball around with my buddies out in the park.

One day, on the soccer field, something pretty wild happened: I bumped into a version of myself from the future. He toll me about how in his time, the digital world had taken over. People were glued to their screens, cooped up in their rooms watching videos, chatting, and sharing stuff. Some kids were even going all out, spending the whole day on electronics without any supervision from their parents, missing out on the chance to make friends and enjoy the great outdoors.

He dropped some truth on me, saying that if we're going to clock in all those hours on our gadgets, we might as well level up our skills, learn the ropes of social media, and you know, why not gear up to make some serious cash in the future using today's tools? Pretty cool, right?

So, here's the deal: get your folks to dive into this book with you. But hey, never lose sight of the real world. Don't forget to soak up the sun, run around, and catch up with your pals. After all, life's not all about screens and buttons!

# CONTENTS

# FROM DAD

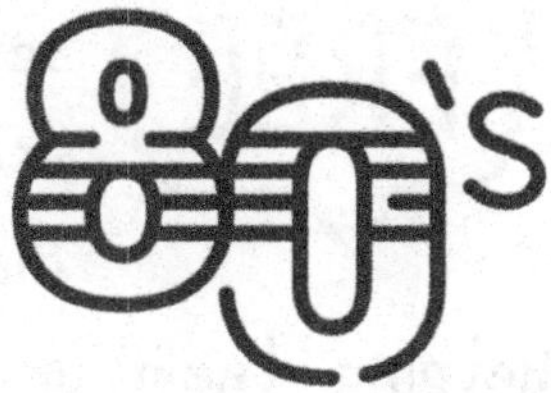


Navigating social networks is a skill many of us born between the '70s and '80s weren't exactly taught. Back in the day, this whole digital communication thing wasn't on the radar. But here's a secret: understanding social networks is necessary, especially if you want to help your kids navigate them smoothly.

In today's world, dodging social media and digital marketing is like trying to avoid your morning coffee, nearly impossible right? As grown-ups, we're bombarded with ads and promotions every time we scroll through our social media feeds. Now, that's one thing for us, but what about our kids? In this age of ever-evolving technology and social media, it's vital to grasp how these platforms can affect our children.

Being a parent in the digital world means more than just setting time limits on screen use. It's about becoming a digital guru for your kids, helping them understand the ins and outs of social media. So, gear up, because in this digital age, being in the know is your superpower as a parent.

Teaching our kids about digital responsibility, setting some boundaries, and encouraging their creativity can be the ultimate toolkit for helping them sail through the **online world safely and responsibly**. But this it's not a one-time lesson; it's an ongoing conversation. It's crucial for us to keep an eye on our child's online activity, not to snoop, but to make sure they're on the right track. Regular check-ins and open, honest chats about their digital footprint go a long way. This way, we guide them to become not just social media users but **responsible digital citizens**.

Now, about Nicolas and his dream of becoming a YouTuber. I get it; it's been on his mind for a while. Social networks are practically ingrained in our lives. We've all been there, posting photos, videos, chatting, and catching up on social events. The digital era is here, and Nicolas wants a piece of the action.

In this book, Nicolas will discuss the importance of teaching other kids about social media and digital marketing, and how to do so responsibly. Sure, social media it's a fun site for creativity and self-expression. The trick is to guide kids in the direction of using it positively, turning it into a playground where they develop not just digital literacy but **also entrepreneurship** and **marketing** skills.

As parents, we've got a key role here. We can guide our children in crafting their own content, managing their social media accounts, and making their digital footprint count for something meaningful.

At the conclusion of the book, you will discover valuable reference sources where you can further explore the information provided. Additionally, a clear and concise glossary has been included to assist you in studying or comprehending any terms used. These special tools have been designed for your benefit, so feel free to utilize them in a manner that best suits your needs!

Introducing entrepreneurship early in their lives isn't just about setting them up for success; it's a crash course in self-reliance. It teaches about online money, the grind of hard work, the bravery in taking risks, the art of learning from mistakes, and the sweet rewards of sticking with it through thick and thin.

So, Nicolas and I are on this journey together. A journey to equip him with **skills that'll be pure gold in the future**. Let's make this learning adventure a game-changer!

# INTRO

My dad has always said that we have to earn our own things with effort and discipline. My older brother jumped on the idea early, kicking off his money-making journey at the ripe age of 13. His first job interview? Well, it was... with Dad. He snagged a gig working alongside Pops, pocketing $25 every Saturday. It meant five hours of grind, but he was stoked because finally, **he could splurge on his own goodies**. Fast forward two years, and he teamed up with his best friend's dad, paving the way to work at a shoe company and then a clothing giant. The guy turned out to be one of the hottest sellers in town. After high school in Miami, he set his sights on Philadelphia to delve into the thing he loved most: architecture. And guess what? He aced it, globetrotting as one of the brightest students. Now, he's rocking the design world, part of a big-shot architectural crew in Philly.

Now, it's my shot at the race. While I might not be hitting 13 yet, I'm all in to kick start my own way as a YouTuber. So, I had to grill my dad on the deets. After some serious back-and-forth negotiations (seriously, it felt like forever!), he gave the green light. And that's why I'm jotting down this book, to tell all the secrets on how to chat up your folks and launch your own digital empire. Of course, it comes with a disclaimer: **adult supervision required**. The internet's a wild place with its good and bad sides. You can whip up mind-blowing stuff and have a blast, but there are hurdles. But hey, if you're serious about chasing those dreams, you gotta put in the elbow grease. I'm gonna spill some tricks on how we kicked off, the whole shebang on growing my YouTube turf. So, buckle up!

Everything has a beginning...

# MY DREAM

During my summer break, I binge-watched the Back to the Future Trilogy with my dad. My absolute favorite was Part II. Marty McFly meeting his future self and snagging a Sports Almanac in 2015 intrigued me. The almanac held 155 pages of sports stats spanning 50 years. Marty's plan was to time travel, hand it to his past self, **and boom!** Instant cash and fame.

Strangely, a similar plot unfolded in my life, well, in this book. One night, mid-dream, I found myself on a soccer field. A standout player caught my eye, and I decided to pick his brain for some soccer wisdom. His advice? Drill and practice like there's no tomorrow. When I questioned his skills, he revealed a wild truth. In his world, folks were glued to their screens via something called vision VR. He was a rare bird who actually stepped outside, connected to the past through this VR magic. According to him,

I had the potential to become the most viral and skilled soccer player of the world, but where he came from, playfields were as scarce as likes and followers in a deserted Facebook page. He had a mission for me: to inspire kids to ditch screens, play sports, and embrace the great outdoors. How? Through **the magic of social media.**

Cue a mission to open a YouTube channel where I'd showcase outdoor activities, soccer, and whatever hobbies rocked my boat. We kicked off a match, him in a slick black shirt, me in blue. As we played, he dished out lessons on social media, how to get my dad's blessing, the ABCs of a digital marketing plan, branding, logo registration, building a webpage, selling on it, and the grand finale: launching and promoting a YouTube channel.

So, as the soccer ball rolled, he broke down what social media is all about.

# SOCIAL MEDIA

# What is social media?

I asked, so he stared with the basics. Social media is the term used to share your thoughts, information and ideas on the internet through **virtual platforms**.

Are gaming sites, also a type of social media? Some of them yes, he replied, for example Roblox, I know you like that game, you can chat with your friends, meet new people, and even donate Robux to other people.

People can use social media on a computer, cellphone, or tablet. Social media platforms are made for people to connect with each other and be part of a **community** and those connections create a **network**.

Depending on the app, your contacts and the people who connect with you, can be called

# friends, followers or subscribers.

There are different types of platforms around social media that I will tell you later, so keep playing.

Many people use social media to **connect** with others for fun, but you can also use it for making money, and to buy and sell stuff.

My Dad dropped a story on me once. When

he was my age, reaching out to a friend meant picking up a phone attached to a wall with a lengthy cord. You had to stay close if you wanted to chat.

Fast forward to today and beyond, and it's a whole new ball game. Everyone's got their own phones, and these little wonders do so much more than just let you talk. The times, they are a-changin'!

# Social Media Platforms

Let me break down the various social media platforms and how they roll. In a nutshell, most social media apps let you share your stuff: photos, videos, and those bite-sized, **reels** or **shorts**.

The heavy hitters include:

## YouTube

YouTube is a free video sharing platform where you can create and upload your own videos and shorts and share them with others.

## TikTok

TikTok is a popular social media app that

allows users to create, watch, and share 15-second videos shot on mobile devices or webcams.

They can add effects like filters, background music, and stickers to the videos, also people can collaborate on content and create split-screen videos even if they are in different locations.

## Instagram

Instagram is a free photo and video sharing app. You can upload photos or videos and share them with your followers or a group of friends. You can also view and comment on posts of friends, share as well as like them.

## Snapchat

Snapchat is a mobile app and is often called Snap by some of its users. It allows you to send pictures or videos to friends. These Snaps vanish after they have been viewed.

## Facebook

Facebook is a social network site that makes it easy for you to connect and share with family and friends.

## ¿Can we use social media?

Yes, he replied, adding a nugget of wisdom. Before diving into any social media, have a heart-to-heart with your folks and chat with your friends' parents or guardians. Why? Well, most social media platforms lay down the age rules, and it's crucial to play by those.

I mentioned to him that, in my view, a good age for watching YouTube is from 3 years old and up, just for watching videos. For instance, they can enjoy "Baby Shark" on YouTube. However, he insists I'm not an expert, suggesting it's better for kids to discuss this with their parents.

I'm aware that if you want to start a channel, you need to do it with your parents or guardians until you turn 13 or older. Discussing social media with your parents or guardians is crucial because, whether you're opening an account or already using one, they should be aware of the social media platforms you're using and the reasons behind it.

**Being responsible and cautious** about the information you share on your social media accounts is essential.

Many, including our parents, believe that social media can be harmful, but there are positive aspects too. I mean, you can create videos showcasing your **favorite activities, hobbies, or skills** and share them with the world. The exciting part is that if a lot of people watch your content, you might even get monetized. It's like getting paid for doing something you love, and that's pretty amazing! However, it requires discipline and persistence. I'll share details on how you can monetize (which means getting paid) in the next chapters!

## Should my parents be involved?

Yes. On any social platform you're thinking of joining, make sure your parents are your first

**friend**, **follower**, or **subscriber**, whether it's YouTube, Facebook, TikTok, or Instagram. This ensures they can keep an eye on your interactions with others. If there's anything you wouldn't want your parents to read or see, it's probably best not to post it on social media.

I totally get if your parents don't let you do some social media, and you feel like you were missing out! Like "everyone else" was on social media having fun without you.

To help you understand why your parents won't allow you to have a social media account, let's talk about the other side for a sec. First, you have to be 13 to have an account with Facebook, TikTok, Instagram, YouTube, and Snapchat. Like, according to the "**terms of service**." The thing, the agreement you sign when

opening an account typically states that if you're 13 or older, you can proceed without any issues. However, if you're under 13, your parents will need to sign up for you. Many kids under 13 have accounts, usually because they've had a conversation with their parents about it.

Sometimes, it's not just about age; your parents might be concerned about social media being a big distraction, taking time away from family or schoolwork, especially if they hold strong but frustrating moral values. They might be worried about cyber-bullying, and that's no joke! Kids like us deal with serious depression over things like who un-friended them or posted secrets about them for everyone to see.

Your parents also might be worried about internet trolls, or people who keep worrying about you and take all the fun out of the social media experience.

These are all understandable concerns for your parents to have, right?

But don't get discouraged!

If you're keen on easing your parents' worries and scoring some social platform freedom, how about teaming up with your dad, mom, or guardian?

Check out the Family Online Safety Institute together.[1] They've got awesome guidelines and even a sample contract tailored for teens like you (ages 13 and under or older). It's a cool way to set some ground rules that everyone's on board with. Also, you could make your own guidelines! Here are some things you might suggest to them.

1 https://www.fosi.org/good-digital-parenting-resource/family-online-safety-agreements

Family Online Safety Institute
GOOD DIGITAL PARENTING

## Family Online Safety Agreement
### Ages 13 and Under

Online safety is a partnership. To make sure everyone stays safe and responsible on the Internet, it's important for kids and adults to agree on the ways that personal devices and technology will be used.

- Share with me/us what you're doing online
- Always be kind, polite, and respectful to others online
- Only access or download music, videos, social apps or gaming accounts with my/our knowledge
- Think before you post a comment, send a chat, or hit the like button. Understand that what you post today will still be there tomorrow and may be there forever
- Only use your device at times that we have agreed on, and respect limits
- Don't access inappropriate content or apps
- Tell me/us if you see bad or disturbing content so we can avoid or report it
- Use security and privacy settings for each account
- I acknowledge that parental controls will be used when needed
- Be a responsible digital user and respect these guidelines for what I am allowed to do online
- Understand the importance of balance and non-tech activities in my life
- Have fun, be creative, and explore safely!

**What other rules are best for our family?**

**I agree to these rules.**

Child's signature Date

I/we agree to support you with these guidelines fairly. I/we agree that the digital world offers plenty of opportunities that I/we would like you to experience, while there are a few risks that I/we must help you avoid.

Parent/Guardian Signature Date

Parent/Guardian Signature Date

For more information:
fosi.org/parenting

I bet your parents would be **seriously impressed** if you take the lead on this. Imagine casually bringing it up yourself.

If they give the green light, awesome! Take a stroll through the account settings together. Ensure your account is always locked down with the strictest privacy settings, visible only to friends you've given the thumbs up to, and do it with your dad, mom, or guardian. **Here's a wise tip**: set up your computer in a central spot. Trust me, if your social media hub is in the living room or your parents' room, it's way less stress for them. No need to worry!

And hey, in the next chapters, I'll deep into Security Apps your parents or guardians can use to keep an eye on things without getting all crazy-parent on you. Stay tuned for the lowdown!

Finally, even if your parents aren't comfortable with sites like Instagram, YouTube TikTok or Facebook, there are also some kid-friendly places to socialize online!

If your parents are still not comfortable with you on any social network sites, I know that could be frustrating. But it won't be forever. Hang in there!

## Is social media safe for us?

Yes, but you have to be careful of strangers though! You cannot give away your private information to strangers but **if you see something you should say something,** tell your parents, teachers, and people that you know so they can help if someone has your personal information. Learn from the content in this book so that you can now understand how to stay safe on social media while also having fun.

Social media has become an essential part of our life as teens and pre-teens, they have given us the ability to be connected to friends and family and are helpful to stay in touch.

However, the downside is that social media platforms come with various threats, and I will outline three of them.

## Cyber-bullying

Cyberbullying involves the use of digital technologies and can occur over devices such as cell phones, computers, and tablets. It takes place through various online avenues, including social media, games, or messaging platforms. This form of bullying is characterized by repetitive behavior that aims to scare, anger, or shame the targeted individuals. It encompasses the sending, posting, or sharing of negative, harmful, false, or mean content about someone else, leading to embarrassment or humiliation.

Cyber-bullying is a form of bullying and adults should take the same approach to address it and protect us from being bullied. Because cyberbullying happens online, responding to it requires different approaches. If you think you are involved in cyber-bullying, there are several things you can do:

**Notice** – Recognize if there has been a change in your mood or behavior and explore what the cause might be. Try to determine if these changes happen around the use of social media.

**Talk** – Talk openly to your parents about it, what is happening, how it started, and who is involved.

**Document** – Keep a record of what is happening and where. Take screenshots of harmful posts or content if possible. Most laws and policies note that bullying is a repeated behavior, so records help to document it.

**Report** – Most social media have clear policies

and reporting processes. If someone is cyberbullying you or someone you know, report it to a family member or the school. You can also contact the app or social media platforms to report offensive content and have it removed. If you have received physical threats, or if a potential crime or illegal behavior is occurring, talk to your parents or guardians and report it to the police.

**Support** – Look for family, friends, and trusted adults who can support you in a situation where negative or hurtful content has been posted on social media.

## Cyberstalking

Cyberstalking is a form of harassment in which individuals use various means to stalk or bully someone, often by exploiting personal information obtained from social media platforms such as Facebook, Instagram, TikTok, and others.

Stalkers can use different techniques to get your private information like spam emails with malicious content, hacking to your social media account and gain your private information using spyware on your computer or other devices or using fake accounts to look like you or someone else.

If you find yourself a victim of cyberstalking, it's crucial to take immediate action. Begin by reporting the offender to their internet service provider (ISP). If this step proves ineffective, consider discussing the situation with your parents and explore the possibility of changing your ISP and all online usernames. For more detailed guidance, consult your internet service provider.

Additionally, it is advisable to block the individual, even if the messages have not es-

calated to explicit threats. Report the offender to the platform you are using, particularly if they are engaging in harassment, stalking, or making threats. Many social media platforms, including Facebook, Twitter, and Instagram, provide user-friendly mechanisms to report abusive behavior.

If the cyberstalking escalates to the point of becoming threatening or alarming, preserve evidence. Take screenshots or save copies of the messages and any relevant interactions. Simultaneously, contact law enforcement to report the situation and provide them with the collected evidence for further investigation.

## Trolls

A troll is an online slang for a person who intentionally tries to instigate conflict, hostility, or arguments in an online social community. Platforms targeted by trolls can include the comment sections of YouTube, Instagram, Facebook, forums, or chat rooms.

Trolls often use provocative messages **to prompt emotional responses** from people. Trolling can occur anywhere that has an open area where people can freely post their thoughts and opinions.

Usually, most people are motivated by positive comments, meaning that they have positive feelings after engaging in an online conversation.

Trolls are different. They have higher levels of something called **negative social potency**. This is my parents' way of saying that they like to cause trouble and distress, along with the attention that causes.

How do you know if you're being trolled? If you are participating in an online discussions or post comments frequently, you may be wondering how to identify trolls or when you're being trolled. There are a few general signs that indicate you may be dealing with a troll.

Trolls will frequently try to attack something you have posted or comment on, like a video, or if you are in favor of something or not. If someone is trying to insult your comment or posts directly, you probably have a troll on your hands.

Another way to spot a troll is by their persistence. When trolls sense that you are getting an emotional response out of you, they usually won't stop until they've gotten you sufficiently riled up.

How to deal with Internet trolls. Now that you know more about what trolling is and how to know if you're being trolled, what should you do if you encounter a troll online?

Typically, the best thing to do is ignore the troll. **Do not engage** this person in an argument or discussion. It is exactly what trolls feed off of because they love the attention.

To report someone for trolling will vary depending on the site you're on. It may be as simple as clicking a Report Button, but if that fails you can usually use a site's "Contact Us" link to send an email letting the site's administrators know about inappropriate behavior from one of the users.

# Setting Boundaries

In social media and digital marketing, it's decisive for parents to establish boundaries for their children. This may involve **restricting screen time**, actively monitoring online activities, and engaging in discussions about what constitutes appropriate content.

**By implementing these boundaries,** parents play a pivotal role in fostering the development of healthy online habits for their children and safeguarding them from potential online risks. Additionally, it is essential to facilitate open and honest conversations about the content children encounter and how it can impact their well-being.

# ¿Can my parents set limits?

Yes, and in addition to setting boundaries and teaching us about digital responsibility, our parents or guardians can also use monitoring and parental control tools to keep us safe online. These tools can help our parents to track our online activity and set restrictions on what we can access. It's important for your parents to regularly check in with you and discuss any concerns or issues that you may have.

# Parental Controls

Parental control software is an app that is downloaded to a master phone (usually a parent's phone), with other apps either secretly (or not so secretly) downloaded to the target (usually, to our phones). The app then tracks, monitors and even secretly screenshots or records our phones with a variety of features to keep parents informed about their children's device usage and online activities.

## Security Apps

My dad uses Bark, which is an app that can block apps and websites or create screen time schedules to help keep their kids safe. Plus, it can monitor text messages, photos, social media, and apps for signs of inappropriate content, depression, cyberbullying and more.[2]" but your parents, or guardians, can choose any app that they consider best for monitoring your online activity.

2 https://www.bark.us/

# NOTES

# DIGITAL MARKETING

# ¿What is Digital Marketing?

Understanding Digital Marketing is easy, just picture the best party ever! You've got a cool idea (product), and you want everyone to have a blast (buy it). So, you design funky invites (ads), create hype (promotions), and make sure the party space is awesome (branding). But, you can make money in the process!

Digital marketing helps **brands** reach their **target audience** and **promote** their **product** or service through your **webpage** or **social media**.

Here are the basics of digital marketing. Keep reading to discover the essential elements that you should start mastering if you're aiming to become a successful online entrepreneur.

**Learning digital marketing isn't rocket science,** but it does require an investment of time, effort, and persistence. So, let's kick off this chapter!

## What is content marketing?

The goal of content marketing is to reach potential customers -people who buy stuff- using content that interests a specific audience. Content is usually published on a website and then promoted through social media, search engine optimization (SEO), or even pay-per-click campaigns.

## What is SEO?

Search engine optimization (SEO) is a way that people or businesses increase visits to

their websites, with the goal of pushing their sites and names to the top of any search results like google. This can occur with search results obtained organically or editorially. When people or companies can successfully apply SEO to their digital marketing strategies, their names and websites become increasingly visible to more consumers.

Imagine a treasure hunt for your favorite online games! So, I know you're a Fortnite pro player, but no one knows you, how can you change that? You search for the right items and clues (words and links) around the map to help others discover your awesome skills and join the match!

## What is SEM?

SEM is like using super speed boosts for Mario Kart! You want to zoom past others and be the champion, right? Search Engine Marketing (SEM) is the turbocharge, using cool ads and tricks to sprint ahead in the race for attention. It's your ticket to victory in the online speedway!

Also referred to as pay-per-click (PPC) marketing. Pay-per-click (PPC) marketing is also a type of online advertising where advertisers pay a fee each time one of their ads is clicked. For example, you are seeing a post or video and there is an ad and you want more information, so you click it. Advertisers bid on the value of a click in relation to the keywords, platforms, and audience type in which it originates.

It's offered primarily by search engines (e.g., Google) and social networks (e.g., Facebook, Instagram and YouTube).

## What is SMM?

Social Media Marketing involves leveraging

popular social networks to build brand identity and achieve marketing goals.

As part of a digital marketing strategy, you can use platforms like Facebook, Twitter, TikTok, Instagram, YouTube to:

1. Post content that targets relevant audiences.

2. Respond to comments, shares, and likes.

3. Launch new products or run promotions and sales.

For example, Mr. Beast uses YouTube to promote his new chocolate bar.

NICOLAS BAHAMON

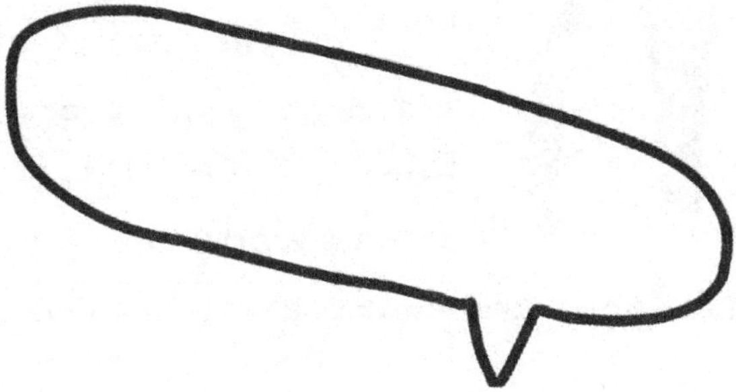

# BRANDING

# What is Branding?

Have you ever seen the big "M" golden arches at the entrance of every Mc Donalds? Or visited Walt Disney World or Disneyland stores? Those are examples of branding.

I have visited Disney World a couple of times, and it was only during my most recent visit that I noticed the Disney logo on every product.

But what is Branding exactly? And why is important? "A brand is a name, term, design, symbol, or any other feature that identifies one seller's good or service as distinct from those of other sellers"[3]

Now, social media branding? It's the process of connecting with your target audience across social media platforms by boosting brand awareness.

3 American Marketing Association.

# What is a logo?

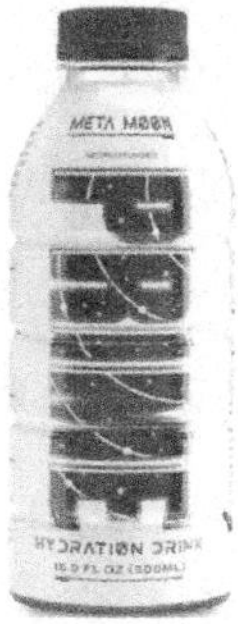

A logo is a graphic symbol used to promote a brand. It can be abstract or figurative design and it may include the name of the brand.

For example, my favorite energy drink is Prime, which was developed by two youtubers Logan Paul and Ksi. There you can see the logo in the bottle.

How are you going to be the coolest kid in the neighborhood if none of the other kids know you? That's the importance of a logo.

# How can you create a logo?

First you have to know your story, why are you creating this brand, then you have to brainstorm some words with your family, and friends, that describe your brand, you must come up with a name for your channel, products or service that stands out and you have to make sure that it is unique if you want to register at a later time. Then sketch some ideas based on those words, show them to your family and friends to see what they think and if they have some comments.

If you have designing skills, you can do it in photoshop, illustrator, or any design software. If you don't have any designing skills, you can ask someone to do it for you or you can hire someone. There are many platforms that you can hire someone to do it for you, the one that I use is called Workana, you can hire a design professional and with your direction the person will design a professional looking logo. I recommend you to look for crazy and fun things to design your brand. Don't use your name or weird word combinations, that's easily forgotten and few will remember you. Let your imagination run wild and come up with a word or logo that totally reflects who you are and what you like.

By creating and using your logo you automatically have the unique rights to use it and to take legal action if someone is using your logo, but by registering your logo or trademark that right is strengthened, and you will have additional protection.

## How to register your logo?

**TM** The trademark symbol ™ signals that the preceding mark is indeed a trademark, specifically an unregistered one. On the other hand, the registered trademark symbol ® is reserved for trademarks that have been officially registered with the appropriate government agency. It's like the difference between claiming a spot and officially putting a flag on it!

Logos and their design may be protected by copyright. There are different organizations available to register a design to give it protection at law. For example, United states Patent and Trademark office (uspto) you can register your logo to a federal level, and trademark it, that is why you see an uppercase "R" in a well-known brand.

You can also register your trademark with the Secretary of State in the state of where you will be using your logo, doing so protects your rights only within that state.

For example, the adidas logo is very unique. As a soccer player I use a lot of adidas products such as cleats, jerseys, socks and shorts. So, you can see the registered mark on top of the "s" because no one can use that logo without their permission, and if they use it, they can be sued for thousands even millions of dollars.

You don't want any other kid to use the logo you created, that's why you need to register it correctly, so that it's yours and only you can use it.

## What is Merchandising?

Merchandising is everything you do to promote and sell your products once the potential customer is in your store. When we talk about merchandise, we are talking about products available for sale, typically in a retail setting.

Merchandising is like the superhero squad

of selling stuff! Picture this: cool strategies, flashy displays, and super discounts team up to make your brand shine. They're on a mission to make customers smile, beat the competition, and turbocharge sales! It's the ultimate power move to grow your brand and stay ahead in the game.

## How can I create and sell my own product?

Before I continue, I would like you to understand what eCommerce is. Imagine a giant online toy store where you can pick and choose the coolest gadgets and games without leaving your room.

Online stores had opened up endless opportunities for entrepreneurs to sell their products online. Whether you have physical goods, digital downloads, or productized services to offer, the online marketplace provides the potential for make money. I will help you understand how you can sell products online, even as a total beginner.

Step 1: Finding the right product to sell is critical right out of the gate because you need something with healthy demand and potential for profit. Conduct thorough market research to identify opportunities, and target markets. Evaluate product ideas based on production costs, pricing potential, shipping considerations, and required upfront investment. Aim to select a product that has existing demand, allows you to differentiate yourself.

Step 2: Choose the right online sales channel, once you have a product, selecting the right online sales channel is crucial to reach your target audience effectively. Here are two things to consider:

1-Build Your Own Online eCommerce Store, creating your custom website for an eCommerce online store gives you the most **control and flexibility** over the shopping experience. WordPress or website-building platforms like Wix offer easy do-it-yourself options.

2-Use Social Commerce Platforms. This allows you to sell directly on social media platforms like Facebook and Instagram Shops.

**Step 3**: Set up an online store, there have never been so many options to start selling products online and building a store with WooCommerce or Shopify and becoming a seller on Amazon.

Step 4: Market your online store, once your online store is set up, you need to market it to attract customers. I will explain later how you can market your online store.

We are almost half-way through this entertaining soccer game. I hope you are enjoying it, and more importantly, that you are learning from the tips and tricks I'm sharing with you. Each recommendation aims to help you make the most of your ideas while also alerting you to potential risks on the internet. Feel free to go back and reread any sections you need for better understanding. I highly recommend doing so before continuing.

Now, we will be delving into concepts that you may not have encountered before, but that doesn't mean we won't make it entertaining.

# NOTES

NICOLAS BAHAMON

# WEBPAGE

# What is a Webpage?

A website serves as the heart of all digital marketing activities, wielding significant power as a crucial channel. Beyond its standalone influence, it stands as the essential platform to execute diverse online marketing campaigns.

Your website plays the pivotal role of representing your brand, product, or service in a way that is not only clear, but also leaves a lasting impression. A seamless online experience is key-ensuring your website is swift, mobile-friendly, and effortlessly navigable. It's not just a page; it's your brand's online home, where clarity and memorability unite.

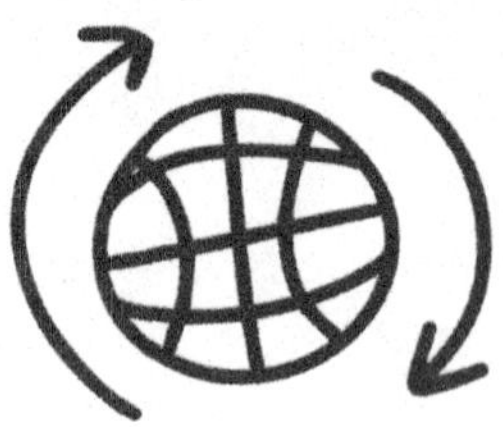

A webpage is a cool **hypertext** document hanging out on the world wide web. It's like a digital robot made up of elements such as text, images, links, videos, and buttons, basically, all the good stuff. These hypertexts are like the secret sauce that connects different parts of the webpage through **hyperlinks**. Think of them as magical portals to other realms!

Now, the real MVP here is the web server. It's like the behind-the-scenes maestro that delivers these web pages to your screen. This software genius understands URLs (those web addresses you see) and the language of the internet, HTTP (the protocol your browser uses to view webpages like https://ChainZd360.com). It's like the ultimate matchmaker, bringing you and your favorite web content together on the vast digital playground.

A web browser takes you anywhere on the internet, letting you see **text, images and video from** anywhere in the world.

A website consists of many web pages linked together under a common domain name, for example ChainZd360.com.

The name "web page" is a metaphor of paper pages bound together into a book. Got it?

People and companies create websites for different purposes, such as:

Posting and finding information on the Web.
Gaining knowledge.
Communicating with each other.
Having fun.

Alright, so let's break down what makes a web page awesome:

**Name of the Website:** Each webpage includes the name of the website or blog. The name of the website and the logo are mostly situated at the top-left corner of the page. It is one of the important components of the webpage.

The website's name also has a link that can redirect to the home page of that site.

A webpage has the following components:

**Navigation Bar:** Think of the navigation bar as the master guide of the webpage. It's like the cool map with links to all the hotspots on your site. You'll find it strutting its stuff at the top or chilling on the left side of the page. Click on any link in that bar, and bam! You're teleported to a new page, just like magic. It's the ultimate sidekick for visitors who want to explore different sections of the website with ease.

**Menu Page:** The menu page is created to show different links of the pages within the webpage. For example, **Home page, About Me, Contact Us,** it can contain as many pages as you want, but these are the most important ones.

**Home Page**: The home page, my friend, is where the magic begins. They call it the 'home' because, well, it's like the launchpad for your web adventure. From here, you've got the keys to go anywhere on the website.

This powerhouse of a page isn't just hanging out; it's loaded with links to all the important zones of the site. It's your personal gateway to **the heart and soul of the website.**

**About-us Page**: This page contains brief information and details of you, products you are selling, or the website. It allows you to know the details of the website you are visiting.

**Contact Page**: This is a simple page made for you to contact me or the website owner. For any issue or any feedback.

**Content of the Page**: Is the information of the page. When you are visiting my webpage, for example, you will see the information contained within the page and it is known as the page's content.

**Paragraphs**: A webpage can have different paragraphs as per their length. The opening paragraph is crucial on the whole page, as it draws the attention of the visitor. If the first paragraph is not interesting and not related to the topic, a user may leave the page immediately.

**Subheadings**: A page may have different subheadings as per the topic, whether related to information about something or a website's web page. Each page should be divided into different subheadings to make it easier for the users to read and understand.

Images: Each webpage contains images to make its content more attractive.

Social Share links: Social share links allow you to share that webpage with their friends on different social sites such as Facebook, Instagram, Twitter, YouTube, etc.

Copyright Info: Each webpage must have Copyright information along with Privacy Policy. This information is available at the end of the page or on the footer of the page.

The data found on a web page is usually in language HTML format.

## What is HTML?

HTML stands for Hyper Text Mark-

**up Language**. Alright, HTML is like the wizard of web page creation. It's the language that speaks in sections, paragraphs, and links, weaving the magic of the internet.

Think of it as the architect's blueprint, using HTML elements, tags and attributes, as the building blocks of a web page. These tags and attributes are the superheroes behind the scenes, shaping the structure and style. It's basically the secret sauce that turns a bunch of code into the awesome web pages you see every day.

Ever remember Tony Stark and his JARVIS computer? Well, guess what? You can have your own webpage that's just as genius! And the best part? You get to be the mastermind behind it, customizing and adapting it to your heart's content. It's like having your own digital playground where you make the rules. How cool is that?

# How I did my website?

Building a website has become a breeze these days, thanks to a bunch of **super-friendly website builders** waiting to be your digital sidekick. It's similar to picking your favorite flavor of ice cream, so many options, so much fun!

With these wizards of the web, you can whip up a stylish website in no time. It's like creating your own little corner of the internet universe. Once you've got a grip on the website you're dreaming of and what it's all about, the next steps become a walk in the digital park. Easy peasy, right?

Choose your Domain name, as we talked before, a domain name is the URL or website address you type into a browser to visit your website, in my case is ChainZd.com, you can type that domain and see what I am talking about.

Here are some tips that I use for choosing a domain name:

Choose one that's easy to spell, avoid abbreviations, relate it to your brand or blog, keep it short and pick a common top-level domain like .com.

You have two choices for registering your domain name: through a domain registrar and your web host, like ionos or website builder like Wix.

IONOS

In my case I did everything with ionos[4]. Often, website builders or web hosting providers offer **free domain name registration** for the first year or just for $1. It's a good idea to check the renewal pricing on both domain registrars and website builders because you may be able to save money in the long term.

---

4 https://www.ionos.com.

Even if one provider is offering a great deal for that first year, you're probably hoping to host your site for the long term. Look for add-on features, including secure sockets layer (SSL) certificates for extra security on your website. On the domain name on your web browser, you will see a lock when the site is secure.

Time to pick your website's VIP suite… I mean, your web hosting provider. They're like the landlords of the internet, giving you a spot in the digital world to store and flaunt your website's files. And guess what? Many website builder services come with hosting packages, making it a one-stop-shop for your digital dreams. Now, if you roll with ionos, it's not just hosting, it's a digital red carpet. They throw in a free SSL certificate, like the cherry on top. Secure and stylish? Count on it!

"Choosing the right web hosting provider is like choosing the right foundation for your house. It's the backbone of your website, so choose wisely. Good hosting speeds up your website which is essential for both user experience and SEO."[5]

Also, you can access some website builders for free, such as Wix. But many features, such as a custom domain, SSL certificate, and the ability to accept online payments, require paid plans.

Alternatively, you could use WordPress to create your website. It gives you more control over the design and functionality of your site, but it requires more technical know-how. To use WordPress, you must choose a hosting service like ionos rather than a website builder.

---

5 Kasper Frederiksen, the Digital Content Specialist for sales software ELISA

With a website builder, you can start customizing your website's design and layout.

**Choose your template.** Templates (or themes) are pre-made designs you can use on your website and fill in with your own content. Choosing the right one comes down to a few key factors.

When you're out there hunting for the perfect one, think about your website's personality. Is it a chill webpage or a bustling online store? Choose a template that gets it, you know?

themeforest

Choose a template that vibes with your brand's aesthetics, and doesn't break the bank (many are free to snag!). Oh, and don't forget the cool factor: go for the ones that resize themselves based on the device, mobile-responsive.

For my website I choose Themeforest[6]. Here's the inside scoop: templates and themes are like the style gurus for your webpage. They're created by the pros, so your site can strut its stuff in style. No need to stress about the color scheme either, most builders make it a breeze to switch things up. Some even throw in pre-built themes with killer color combos, like they read your mind or something.

Now, my dad and I are diving into the HTML language, so we snagged an HTML template to jazz up our site. But guess what? You've got options galore, whether you're rolling with Shopify, gearing up for some ecommerce action, or rocking the WordPress vibes. Pick a theme, sprinkle in your own magic, and watch

6 https://themeforest.net

your webpage come to life.

And hey, if the tech stuff feels like a maze, don't sweat it. Team up with your parent or guardian, **make it a duo mission!** Or, if you're on the lookout for a web wizard on a budget, hit up Workana. There are friendly experts out there just waiting to help on your webpage dream.

If you want to sell, add e-Commerce to your website. While this is an optional step, it's likely a popular one – a major reason behind wanting to build a website is that you want to promote or sell something -.

Most web hosting services offer packages and upgrades to add a storefront to your website.

If you know or want to learn software to build webpages, I will recommend Dreamweaver by Adobe. This software is great for code and changing the HTML code on a template but will involve more technical knowledge. Once you download the template from Themeforest, they come with well-documented instructions of how you can change and modify the webpage. **So, you've got your logo shining**, content popping, and images on point, you're practically in the website hall of fame. The big moment is around the corner: publishing time!

Now, here's something more: every website builder adds its own twist to the publishing party. It's like the grand finale, and each one's got its own special fireworks. So, prepare and get ready to launch your masterpiece into the digital galaxy. The world is about to see what you're made of!

# Can I sell stuff from my webpage?

Yes. There are several ways to build an online store. You can create a website and add a shopping cart plug-in. Also, you can choose an e-commerce platform, like Shopify or Square, which are like online store website builders.

Also, you can sell a product on an e-commerce platform or an online marketplace such as Etsy, Amazon or Facebook.

Promoting yourself on social media can help you drive traffic to your ecommerce store, build brand awareness, and connect directly with potential customers. By posting regularly and replying to user comments, you can build a connection with the millions of people who use social media. You Can do this through Youtube, TikTok and Instagram.

# NOTES

# YOUTUBE

## My YouTube channel.

I kicked off my YouTube journey with this dream of becoming a YouTuber. Watching videos from awesome creators like Mr. Beast, Airrack, Ryan Trahan, Preston, and more got me super inspired. So, I pitched the idea to my mom and dad to see if I could give it a shot. Obviously not on Mr. Beast's level, but my own channel with some cool stuff to share.

**Once my parents gave the green light** and we set some ground rules, we sat down together to brainstorm. You know, throwing around ideas and figuring things out. We nailed down the basics and talked about the videos we wanted to make, why we were doing it, and who our audience would be. It took us a couple of weeks, but it was necessary to understand why I wanted to make videos.

In the beginning, we shot videos in different spots, chatting about various things. Then, like a bolt of lightning, it hit me: **soccer is my absolute passion!** That lightbulb moment sparked the decision to center my channel on soccer, showcasing my daily training, tutorials, and even some game highlights. The idea? To inspire kids to flaunt their passions and maybe even spark some business ideas. The journey has been a thrill, and I'm stoked to share it with everyone!

Then we stablished the core principles, like my dad said, but in simple words, what is going to be my channel about, so we defined what my channel is about and designed a brand that mirrors my vision, something that brings people together on a peaceful and deeper level. And voila, ChainZd was born (Chain, Zen Deep), the brand.

Once we had our brand locked in, it was logo-design time. But here's the deal: everything we did leading up to this point wasn't about getting it perfect. No analysis paralysis here. We just needed a solid understanding of the brand we were bringing to our audience.

Then came the moment of truth: making videos. We published our first video, diving into how I kicked off my YouTube journey and why ChainZd.

Smooth sailing, right? Well, not for long. Before we knew it, we hit our first major roadblocks. But before tackling that, we needed to prep the thumbnail and title for our video.

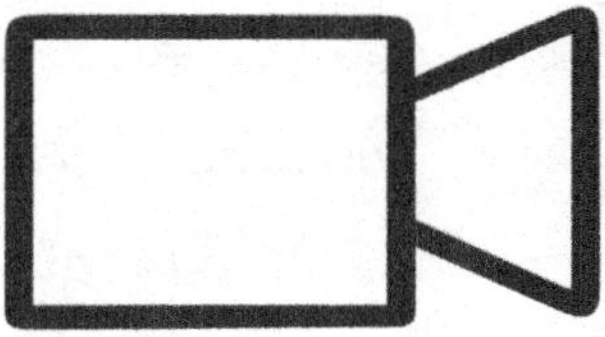

Choosing the right thumbnail and title proved to be a challenge. I wanted to tell the story of how I embarked on this journey **and made the first video.** It took us more than five hours to create a video that's less than five minutes, but for our debut, it finally felt good. Editing came next, and with my dad's help, it went better than expected. Most importantly, we all learned from the process. Now, it's time to hit upload and see where this journey takes us!

## How can you open and post videos on YouTube?

Countless small channels are blowing up on YouTube right now and there has never been a better time to start your own channel. Like most social media platforms, you can set up your account with a **username, picture and a profile**. You'll need a Google account to sign in to YouTube. Your parents or guardians can create a Google account for you if you are under 13 (or the applicable age in your country) and manage it using a Family Link. That way you can get access to Google products like Search, Chrome, and Gmail, and your parents or guardians can set up basic digital rules to supervise you.

Once you've signed in, the YouTube homepage will appear, and you'll see trending and popular videos recommend for you, and more. If you see a video you want to watch, just click it to start playing.

**Social media profile picture**. Your profile picture may seem like a small detail, but in the world of social media branding, it's a big player. Here's the deal: Make sure that every social media profile picture flaunts your logo. Why? Because that logo is your superhero cape, creating a sense of unity across all platforms. It's like your digital signature, making it a breeze for users to spot your channel in the vast sea of search results.

Now, some folks go straight into content creation, overlooking the power of a snazzy profile. But let me spill a little secret: it's one of the easiest ways to give your YouTube channel a promotional boost and sprinkle some magic on your SEO. (And yeah, do you remember what SEO is?) So, don't sleep on the profile game: it's your channel's first impression, after all.

**Social Media Bio.** This section should contain a summary of what you do and what it offers to your visitors. Some social media platforms offer more space for your bio than others, but you don't want to overwhelm visitors when they first get to know you. Try to limit your bio sections to two or three sentences.

Look at my YouTube bio as an example.

Here are some practices for creating an effective YouTube profile:

**Be consistent.** Use a similar color palette, writing style, and layout as you do on your website and other social channels.

**Optimize your channel description.** This is a great place to add keywords like, sports, funny stuff, challenges or whatever you like to post. That will keep viewers coming back for more.

**Ask this.** How often will you post new content? Let subscribers know your schedule, then make sure you stick to it.

**Include your contact info.** Nothing private though! Just an email, you never know who might want to reach you. Make it easy for them and you could land some great partnerships.

Here's what you should consider when writing your YouTube video descriptions:

Front-load your keywords in the description and title.

**Have the most important information** in the first 100 to 150 words, which appears above the "SHOW MORE" button.

**Develop a posting schedule.** After you've locked in your social media platforms, it's time to craft the perfect posting schedule. This schedule is like your content compass, steering the ship through the digital sea. It's not just about when you post; it's about the rhythm and flow of your online presence. So, buckle up, because your posting schedule is about to dictate a whole bunch of awesome things, including:

- What kinds of content you post.

- How often you post.
- What time of the day you post.
- What's included in the post.

While these factors might shimmy and shake a bit across platforms, one thing remains constant: optimize those posts! It's the secret sauce to reaching as many visitors as humanly (or algorithmically) possible. So, get ready to sprinkle some digital magic on your content and let it shine across the online universe.

One last thing

**Get verified on YouTube.** If you have 100,000 or more subscribers, you can apply to be verified on YouTube.

You don't need to be verified to be successful on YouTube but having that extra stamp of credibility will only help your channel grow.

## Creating engaging content and storytelling techniques

Storytelling isn't just a tool; it's the superhero cape of content creation. It's the magical thread that weaves a connection with your audience, inspiring and persuading them to dive headfirst into your content.

When you're on the journey of crafting engaging content, always keep your audience in the spotlight. Here are a few tips and storytelling techniques to keep your content game strong:

**Know your audience,** what are their interests, what do they need or want to know? Once you understand your audience, you can make or adapt your content and stories to their needs.

**Be clear and concise.** Your stories should be easy to follow and understand. Get to the point quickly and avoid using unnecessary expressions.

**Evoke emotions.** Use humor, sadness, anger, and other emotions to connect with your audience on a deeper level.

**Make your stories relevant.** Relate your stories to your audience's lives and experiences. This will help them connect with your message and make your stories more memorable.

**Use vivid language.** Use descriptive language to paint a picture for your audience and help them imagine your stories.

**Be yourself.** Let your personality shine through your writing. This will help build trust with your audience and make them more likely to engage with your content.

Tell stories of overcoming adversity. These stories can inspire your audience and give them hope. They can also teach your audience valuable lessons about perseverance and resilience.

**Be funny.** A little bit of humor can go a long way in making your content more engaging. It can also help to lighten the mood and make your audience more receptive to your message.

**Use personal anecdotes.** Dishing out personal stories is like opening a secret door to connect with your audience on a whole new level. It's your battle pass, revealing that you're not just a content creator; you're a fellow human who gets the struggles and triumphs. However, remember, this isn't an open diary session. Let's keep it engaging and relatable without turning it into your personal chronicle!

**Use visuals.** Images, videos, and infographics can help to make your content more visually appealing and engaging. They can also help to break up your text and make it easier to read.

**Ask questions.** Asking questions can help to engage your audience and get them involved in the conversation. It can also help you to learn more about your audience and what they're interested in.

By following these tips, you can create engaging content and storytelling that will connect with your audience and make a lasting impact.

# How to promote your channel?

Alright, we're entering into the YouTube galaxy, the second most-visited spot on the web, boasting a whopping 2.1 billion users worldwide! If you're eyeing that platform's potential, mastering the art of promoting your channel is a game-changer.

Now, when folks vibe with your video, they can do more than just watch. They can hit the like button, drop a comment, share the love, and even subscribe to your channel for more goodness. And here's the cool part: as they keep diving into your topic on YouTube, the algorithm gets in on the action. It starts serving up your videos on their home screen, creating a sweet cycle of content love.

**Ready for some YouTube wizardry?** Here are a few of my favorite tricks to sprinkle some optimization magic on your content, making sure new folks discover the awesomeness of your channel:

Be consistent with your branding.

**Choose Google-friendly keywords.** A great YouTube channel starts with great SEO. And great SEO starts with understanding what users are searching for.

There's no set rule for which keywords will help your YouTube video rank well.

Here's how to find a Google-friendly keyword for any video.

Use concise and descriptive video titles. The title is the first thing users see when they find your content.

Here are some basic tips for writing strong YouTube titles:

**Keep it short**. The most popular YouTube videos tend to have the shortest titles. Stick to 60 characters or less or some of your title may get cut off when displayed.

**Identify possible keywords**. Stash your keywords in the first half of your title. Why? Because in the online reading game, most eyes lock onto the beginning, and the rest might just slip through the cracks. Don't let that valuable information go unnoticed!

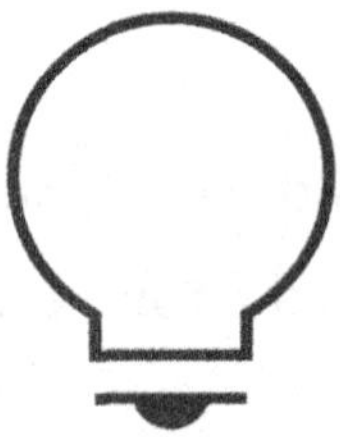

But hey, let's talk about engagement—it's not just grabbing attention. It's about turning heads and getting those clicks. The crème de la crème of headlines? They don't just sit pretty; they offer a clear benefit or stir up an emotional rollercoaster. It's the art of making readers go 'Aha!' or 'Wow!' and clicking that link faster than you can say 'YouTube sensation.' Now, that's the magic of a killer headline!

**Create custom thumbnails.** Here's a pro-tip: Thumbnails? They matter, maybe even more than titles. Why? Because our brains are wired to be visual creatures, and a striking image can do wonders. Now, YouTube may whip up automatic thumbnails, but let's face it, they can be a bit... meh. To skyrocket those views, go into any design software and craft a custom thumbnail that screams, 'Click me!' Trust me, your audience will thank you for the eye candy.

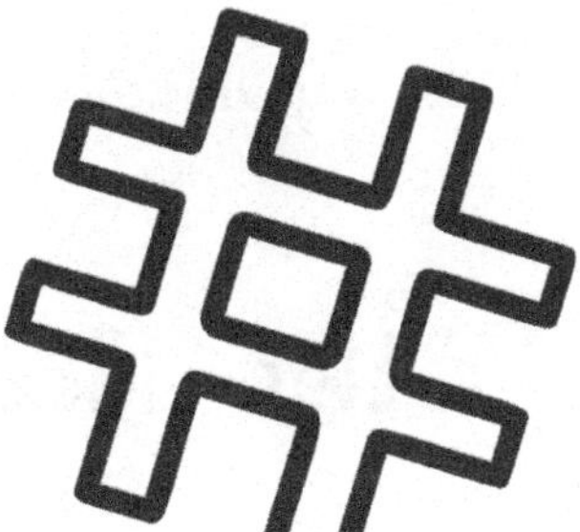

Include a few relevant hashtags in your title and description. Be sure to follow YouTube's **hashtagging (#)** rules before you post.

You can also mention keywords in the video itself. But just like with text, people lose attention quickly. Use a couple of keywords during a brief intro for best results.

Add one or multiple categories to help YouTube understand who to recommend your video to. It's like telling YouTube, "Hey, this video is for the cool teens. They need to see this!"

Great content is the best way to keep viewers engaged and the most effective way to rank well in YouTube search. That's because YouTube's ranking system prioritizes the viewer's experience.

Before you publish any video, ask yourself:

**What problem does this video solve?**

**Is it entertaining?**

**Create high-quality videos.** Even the most outstanding content can take a hit from poor video quality. It's crucial to give your content a professional touch before hitting that post button. Grab your smartphone, run a quick soundcheck before hitting record, and consider picking up some basic editing skills. Don't worry if you're not a born filmmaker, everyone starts somewhere.

**Interact with your subscribers.** Real engagement doesn't end at content creation. The most successful YouTubers constantly monitor and interact with their Subscribers.

**Respond to viewers' comments** –even the negative ones but be careful with trolls – and "heart" your favorites. Use analytics to identify your top fans and show them some extra love.

**Try a Q&A.** Audience Q&As are one of the most effective ways to build a community on YouTube. Ask your subscribers to send you questions by comment or tweet. Then create a video to address them.

By showing your subscribers that they matter, you'll boost watch time, view counts, and engagement.

Run contests. Contests are another great way to get your audience involved. With a single video, you can collect viewer data, encourage likes or comments, and gain subscribers.

**Please respect YouTube's contest rules and restrictions.**

**Be active in the community.** YouTube is all about finding your niche and building your following within it.

**Subscribe to channels** that target a similar audience to you. Watch, like, and share their content. Leave thoughtful comments or mention them in your own videos.

Not only will this give you a better sense of what your competition is up to, it can also help you reach new viewers.

## Work with (the right) influencers.

Expanding your reach is a walk in the park when you team up with influencers. YouTube personalities, in particular, open doors to already active and dedicated communities. Plus, they're your go-to resource when creativity hits a roadblock.

Ensure your chosen influencers mirror the values of your brand. Ask yourself: does a partnership make sense, and will it bring value to your audience? If the answer is no, keep searching. Remember, inauthentic content can do more harm than good.

Do not forget! Here's one golden rule to any successful partnership: **Be authentic.**

## Respect YouTube's community guidelines

YouTube is cracking down hard on inappropriate content due to a rising number of underage users.

Don't post anything you wouldn't want your parents or your little sister to see, otherwise, your video will get flagged and removed from YouTube.

**Create a series.** Consistency pays off, believe me. Post videos on a regular schedule to keep viewers coming back to your channel again and again.

Choose a catchy, keyword-friendly name for your series and create a custom thumbnail to give each video in the series a similar look and feel.

**Add your videos to your playlist.** Videos in a playlist are more likely to appear in YouTube's Suggested Videos column. Plus, playlist titles are a great place to add keywords.

Add a call-to-action. (CTA), Maybe you want to push your viewers to like or share your video. Maybe you want them to click through to your website. Whatever the "ask," the best CTAs are always clear, compelling, and urgent.

YouTube has a call-to-action extension for in-stream ads. But there are also lots of free ways to add CTAs to videos:

**Talk to your audience.** Look into the camera and verbally tell viewers what you want them to do.

**Video descriptions.** Ask viewers to comment, share, or like your video in the description itself.

**End card.** Add a customizable screenshot to the beginning, middle, or end of the video to boost subscriptions.

**Cross-promote your channel.** Connect with audiences beyond YouTube to establish a community around your channel. Explore ways to integrate videos into your blog or other social media platforms.

Ensure your brand maintains a consistent look and feel across all platforms. Additionally, vary your captions with each post to keep things fresh.

Numerous imaginative strategies exist for promoting your YouTube channel without resorting to repetitive messages. Here are some straightforward ideas to kickstart your efforts:

**Blogging.** Does your website have a blog? Embed videos in your posts, along with searchable transcriptions. This will increase both video and page views.

You can also use your blog to generate new content and ideas for your channel. Use Tube Buddy Analytics or VidIQ to find which posts get the most traffic. And see if there is a way to create a video on that topic?

Embed the end result into the post itself. This will add value to your blog while encouraging readers to check out your YouTube channel.

I recommend using a simple icon rather than a long, sad-looking URL.

Maximize your promotional efforts by not only showcasing your videos but also actively advocating for new subscribers. Embed links to your channel wherever possible. This not only boosts your visibility in YouTube searches but also elevates your ranking on Google. Additionally, take advantage of the YouTube Community post feature to promote your videos.

**Your YouTube Community** tab functions similarly to a Facebook or Twitter feed, allowing you to share video announcements, polls, questions, and other engaging content with your audience.

Emulate the strategies of your favorite YouTubers. Chances are, you began your YouTube journey as a subscriber to channels you admire. Identify successful channels that align with yours and observe their practices for inspiration.

I use a tool called Tubebuddy[7] app, where you have a tile generator and can generate new ideas, you can add chapters to your videos, find useful tags and other option to optimize your video, but if you don't have it, do not worry, choose a keyword that prioritizes video and suits your content Then, put your own spin on it.

Find out what works (and do more of it)

## YouTube's analytics are powerful. Use them wisely!

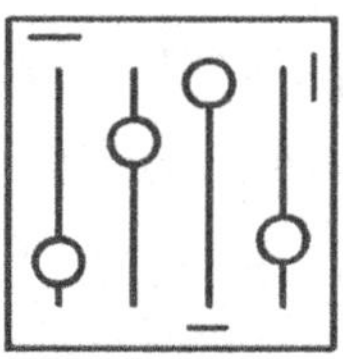

Take a dive into your data to understand your audience on a deeper level. How old are they? What languages do they speak? Which video styles do they prefer? Use this information to create content that truly captures their interests.

---

7 https://www.tubebuddy.com/pricing?a=ChainZdTubebuddy

# Building an online presence and personal branding

Thinking about diving into the world of social media but not sure where to begin? With millions of users joining these platforms daily, there's an incredible opportunity to gain exposure. Yet, your success on social media is directly tied to the effort you put in. How well you articulate your ideas can significantly impact the results you'll achieve.

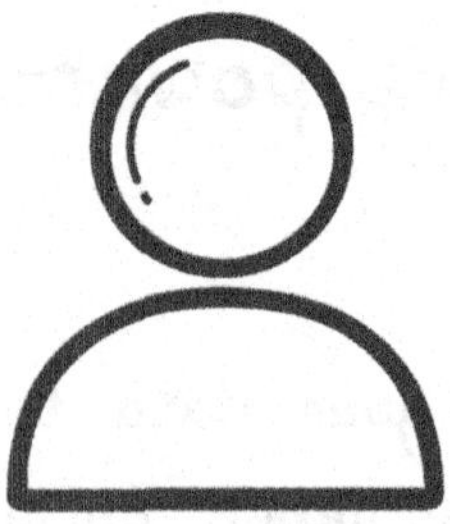

That's precisely why my dad and I crafted this book, to provide you with insights into digital marketing and its connection to social media. Now that you've got a grasp of the basics of branding, you're ready to establish a strong brand presence and elevate your profile.

The starting point? A well-thought-out social media branding plan.

Having a plan in place allows you to streamline the process, increasing your chances of grabbing attention and achieving your goals. Whether you're navigating YouTube or Instagram, your social media branding plan should be adaptable to every platform you choose.

## Is being active on social media worth it?

The short answer is yes. The audience you're trying to reach is another major component to consider before jumping into social media. You need to think about what they're expecting to see from you and how they'll react, and what they prefer to see.

Learning about your target audience can provide you with key information that will input on your social media branding plan. Here are some things you should know about your audience:

- Their age ranges.
- Their likes and dislikes.

When you have a clear idea of your brand and your target audience, you can start with social media branding.

- Branding yourself on social media.
- Complete your social media profile.
- Use the correct social media platforms for your brand and audience.
- Develop a posting schedule.
- Interact with your audience.
- Integrate your website into your social media presence.

Establishing your brand on social media is all about connecting with your target audience and effectively communicating why your brand deserves their attention. Now, let's explore some strategies to enhance your brand presence on social media.

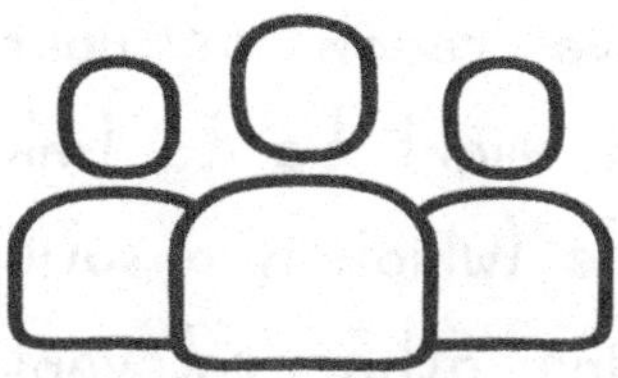

By now, you should have a **clear understanding** of how to optimize your profile. It's time to transform your profiles into a cohesive brand narrative through visually engaging content in the form of images and links.

To round out your social media branding plan, it's crucial to bridge the gap between your social media presence and your website. A simple yet highly effective way to achieve this is by incorporating a link in your profiles. Personally, I make sure to have a link on all my social media accounts, accompanied by a note at the end of each profile stating, "Managed by Parents." This serves as a reassurance to everyone that your parents have your back.

Linking users from social media to your website not only strengthens your brand's online presence but also emphasizes the extensive reach of your brand. While the instinct might be to link directly to your homepage (which is a solid choice), consider featuring other relevant pages or showcasing your latest blog posts for a dynamic and engaging user experience.

Consider each social media platform's (described at the beginning of the book) advantages and disadvantages, then decide which best suits your brand needs.

Remaining consistent, keep in mind your posts' frequency and type of content, that will help develop your branding in the eyes of your users.

Interact with your audience. It's not enough

to build a great profile and post helpful content consistently. You need to interact and engage with your audience regularly as we talked before.

Social media platforms such as YouTube are purposefully designed to foster interaction, and the more actively you engage, the greater the likelihood of platform promotion for your posts. Demonstrating responsiveness on these platforms not only builds rapport with your audience but also conveys trustworthiness and credibility, key factors for both current and potential followers.

To truly amplify your brand presence on social media, it's essential to seamlessly integrate your website into your platform strategy. Why? While social media does provide selling functionalities, your website remains the paramount tool for conversion. As discussed earlier, a pivotal first step is sharing a link to your website in your bio.

This strategic move not only directs your audience to a central hub of comprehensive information but also positions your brand for optimal conversion opportunities. Social media serves as a dynamic showcase, but your website stands as the ultimate destination for a deeper and more meaningful interaction with your brand.

LET'S GO !

# YOUTUBER

# What is and how to be an Influencer?

Imagine Batman being like a superhero influencer. You know how he's always doing cool stuff to make Gotham City better? Well, if he keeps all his awesome bat-moves a secret, no one in the city would know about them, right?

Being an influencer is a bit like that. Batman wants to show everyone the cool things he can do, just like influencers want to share the cool stuff they like with their friends. If Batman tells everyone about the great gadgets he uses, more people in Gotham might want to be like him or help him out.

Similarly, influencers share what they love, whether it's video games, fashion, or cool gadgets, with their friends.

The definition of influencer, and what it means to be one, is constantly evolving regarding what types of content influencers share on social networks and how they share it. Influencers can range from YouTube gamers to people who post detailed how-to videos. Even with this variety, there are some consistencies:

Influencers don't have to be celebrities in order to succeed. Being influencer is possible without already being a public figure. Even though influencers can attract online audiences into the hundreds of thousands and even millions, they may not consider themselves "celebrities" in offline settings.

Influencers possess the potential to fuel business growth. The strength of being an influencer lies in the type of marketing that's achievable. You can attract attention from social media users and brands that will pay you to promote their products in influencer marketing campaigns, all thanks to the connections you've forged with their target audiences.

Becoming an influencer can be an exhilarating journey. You'll get the chance to inspire your audience, share your passions, and generate some income.

Complete basic tasks, an important first step in starting your influencer brand is to approach it like you would a business. By adopting business approaches, you can attract your target audience.

Articulate your influencer goals, such as building a following around your passions and hobbies working with specific brands you admire.

Write a summary of what kind of influencer brand you want to create, including the topics you want to post about, the aspects of yourself you want to share (affiliate links, sponsored social media posts, etc.).

Identify your niche, a niche is a highly specific market segment of consumers that an influencer can market to online. Your niche can be based on a category of content that you'd share on social media as well as the demographics (age, location, income, etc.) and psychographics (values, beliefs, interests, etc.) of your target audience.

To gain a clear understanding of your niche, take a moment to reflect on what truly sparks your passion. Consider your hobbies, the content that captivates you, and what you envision creating yourself. Look at the influencers who already inspire you—those who have found success in your field. Take note of the social media users drawn to these influencers and the specific platforms they engage on. Explore the range of products you genuinely love and would be excited to promote to others.

**Get to know your audience.** Once you've identified your niche, conduct market research to understand your audience. That way, you can develop a lasting connection with your audience and post valuable content that satisfies their interests and goals. Click around on social media to find out the type of comments your audience makes on other social media influencers' content.

**Create your influencer brand.** Consider your influencer brand as a cohesive representation of your personality, values, and passions, establishing authority on a specific topic. This brand serves as a foundation to explore your business potential. Take a moment to define the impression you aim to make on your online audience and what you want to be recognized for.

You might opt to craft an aesthetic for your influencer brand, incorporating distinct colors, fonts, and a consistent brand voice. This deliberate approach will not only enhance your online presence but also contribute to a memorable and authentic representation of yourself in the digital landscape.

**Explore your content strategy.** A large part of an influencer brand is the content you share on social media channels. Make a list of individual pieces of content that explore different facets of your category.

Consider establishing a content creation calendar to guide the timing and format of your posts. For instance, you might dedicate Mondays to sharing insights into your morning routine, host live "Ask Me Anything" sessions on Wednesdays, and reserve Fridays for educational tutorials.

**Optimize your online presence,** before officially launching your influencer brand and posting content in earnest, take time to optimize your online presence as a whole, so that you can build brand equity. Your online presence can include:

Creating new social media accounts for your

influencer brand or converting your existing accounts into influencer accounts.

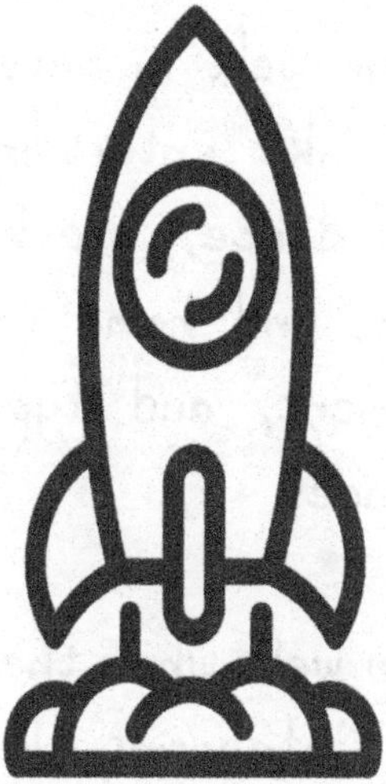

Select your channels. Along with optimizing your online presence, you need to select the social media platforms and marketing channels through which you'll influence and inspire an audience. Being selective about your channels offers two main advantages. One, you can focus your efforts on mastering the features of one or two channels. And two, you can choose the platform or channel that works best for the type of content you share.

Here are some general differences between platforms:

YouTube Influencers tend to perform well when promoting products that require an explanation or video tutorial to use.

TikTok influencers perform well in categories like entertainment, dance, pranks, fitness, and home improvement, and typically cater to Gen-Z audiences.

Instagram influencers perform well when their content leverages imagery. Categories that are popular on Instagram include fashion, beauty, food, travel, and fitness.

Post unique content on a regular basis. Once you've set up your online presence and selected the channels and platforms on which you'll appear, it's time to start posting content. Bear in mind that it can take time to see tangible results from your content efforts; consistency is key.

Engage your audience. While you post regular content on social media, engage with members of your audience to increase your "know, like, and trust" factor. Here are some engagement methods:

Like, comment on, and repost content by your followers and fellow influencers in your niche.

Respond to comments on your posts.

Start conversations on social media by asking your audience questions about their interests and opinions.

Message your most engaged followers to ask them what kind of content they'd like to see you create.

Collaborate with other brands. As your social media presence gains attention, attracting followers and becoming a go-to for entertainment or information, brands might reach out to collaborate with you. You can also take the initiative and pitch to brands directly. To maximize these opportunities and align them with your goals, get ready by completing the following tasks:

Prepare for these opportunities in advance, so that you can earn income and work with brands in a way that aligns with your goals, by completing the following tasks.

Make a list of the brands you'd like to collaborate with.

Decide how you want to collaborate with

them, including sponsored posts and affiliate marketing, as well as how you want to monetize your efforts.

Draft a description of content that you can create to promote various products that you can use for your website or for contacting brands via email or messenger.

Draft a template for pitching these brands directly.

Refine your influencer skills and strategy. As your list of followers and brand collaborators grows, commit to the regular upkeep of your influencer business:

Set aside time periodically to conduct research into new influencer tools and techniques, social media platforms' latest features, and how your audience is behaving online.

Take note of which content gets the most engagement from your audience and be willing to adjust your content strategy accordingly.

Stay connected to your audience and seek to understand their interests, goals, and challenges more intimately.

## Creators' vs Entrepreneurs

Entrepreneurs are individuals who initiate and manage their own businesses, fueled by innovative ideas. They dream big, exude passion for their endeavors, work tirelessly, and persevere through challenges. Without entrepreneurs, there would be a lack of innovation, hindering the birth of transformative ideas capable of shaping the world, generating employment, and boosting the economy. Fortunately, a new generation of young individuals stands ready to tackle global issues and find solutions.

On the other hand, content creators invest their time in crafting, editing, and sharing content for their audiences. In a way, content creators can be considered entrepreneurs. They may develop and sell their own content, such as videos, music, or writing, and monetize it through advertising or other channels.

Before delving into what it takes to be a content creator, it's essential to clarify the distinctions between being a hobbyist and having a strategic plan, as well as between a content creator and a content entrepreneur. In our current era, even an 11-year-old excelling on YouTube can be considered a content creator. However, there's a crucial nuance: if the young creator is not only generating content but also earning money for their work, they truly fall into the category of a content creator. Moreover, if they apply strategic planning to build a business model, then they can be deemed a content entrepreneur.

Becoming a content entrepreneur involves more than just a viral piece of content. Many creators and influencers experience a single viral hit and then fade into obscurity. The real work happens long before that point. So, if your goal is to evolve from an online content creator to a content entrepreneur, I recommend putting in the hard work, implementing effective marketing strategies, and following the guidance provided in this book.

READ MORE

# Are you ready to be a Content Entrepreneur?

Content creation is a relatively new industry, did you know that "content creator" is one of the most searched professions on Google? However, creators encounter many of the same challenges as other startup entrepreneurs. Take YouTubers like Mr. Beast, who began creating videos at home, and before he knew it, he was making money. The next question becomes, how do you grow and manage this newfound venture?

Whether you're a sports enthusiast or a gamer, there's no straightforward and objective answer to determine if you're ready to adopt an entrepreneurial mindset. It goes beyond page views or revenue metrics. The key lies in delving deep within yourself: Is this purely for fun, or do you genuinely aspire to turn your passion into a full-time career?

Do you want to maintain it as a hobby? If so, that's perfectly fine and commendable. There's no universal method to decide whether to transition from hobbyist to entrepreneur, but it remains a conscious decision.

The moment you decide, "I want to start earning by doing this," you shift from being a hobbyist to an entrepreneur. Now, it's about approaching it with the right mindset.

What happens next?

With an entrepreneurial mindset, content entrepreneurs set themselves up for success, building strategy and intention around their every decision.

Now have the tools to identify great – and not-so-great – opportunities, as creators we are dedicated to craft and produce beautiful work.

Content entrepreneurs wield influence over the tone, quality, and substance of their work. However, lacking a business mindset could lead to unprofessionalism—missing deadlines, lacking creative dedication to content, and potentially missing out on future opportunities.

As you construct your brand, remember you're not navigating this journey solo. It's the juncture where success dawns, and you find yourself questioning, 'How is this possible?' Just so you know, these career paths were likely unimaginable for our parents at our age.

Regardless of your success, maintaining focus and humility is crucial. The moment you start feeling like you've reached the summit, a reality check is likely in order, because that realization is a truly exceptional thing!!!!!

Now it's your turn, a new digital journey awaits! Picture yourself as a superhero, ready to take on the world. Begin by having a chat with your parents or guardians. Brainstorm some cool ideas, come up with a name, and a logo, that represents you, this is the birth of your personal brand.

Next, deep into the online world by launching your very own website. Claim your space on the internet and let it be a reflection of your unique self. Consider opening up a YouTube channel where you can showcase your passions, hobbies, and what you excel at. Who knows! You might even make some money along the way!

Remember, the key ingredients for success in this digital adventure are discipline and dedication. Stay committed to your journey, and you'll be amazed at what you can achieve.

Go ahead, start your digital adventure and let the world see the amazing person you are!

Subscribe

# Thank you for reading my book!

# ACKNOWLEDGMENTS

I want to express my heartfelt gratitude to my dad, whose unwavering support and guidance played a key role in bringing this book to life. Without him, it wouldn't have gained the popularity it has today.

A special shoutout to my mom, who gave me the unique and memorable name, ChainZd. Thanks to my brother for generously sharing his life experiences, which enriched the content of this book.

I extend my thanks to David Herrera for his incredible design work, and to Alexander Estrada for his valuable contributions to the project. A big shoutout to my dear friend Josua and his family who not only taught me the ropes of soccer, but also inspired me along the way.

Last but not least, a sincere thank you to my

audience. Your interest and support are what make this journey worthwhile. I genuinely appreciate each and every one of you for making this dream a reality.

# SOCIAL MEDIA GLOSSARY

Abbreviation: A shortened form of a written word or phrase used in place of the whole word or phrase. "USA" is an abbreviation of "United States of America."

Abstract design: Is a type of art that uses shapes, colors, forms, and gestural marks to create a work that does not attempt to depict visual reality accurately.

App: Software designed to run on a mobile device.

Audience: In marketing, the target audience is the group or segment within that target market that is being served advertisements. audience may be dictated by age, gender, income, location, interests or a myriad of other factors.

Bio (biography): A short description about someone.

Blog: An informal and regularly updated webpage written by an individual or group (called a blogger)

Brand recognition: Is the ability of consumers to recognize an identifying characteristic of one company versus a competitor.

Digital Footprint: Is the information about a particular person that exists on the internet as a result of their online activity.

eCommerce: Is a method of buying and selling goods and services online.

Entrepreneurship: Is when an individual who has an idea, does that idea real, usually to disrupt the current market with a new product or service.

Evergreen Videos: Refers to videos that remain relevant and valuable to viewers over an extended period, often for years or even indefinitely. These types of videos are not tied to a particular event or trend and can be watched and enjoyed by viewers regardless of when they were published.

Going viral: when content is shared rapidly across social media.

Hashtag: A word or phrase preceded by a # symbol, to identify content on a topic

Leveraging: Refers to the use of debt (borrowed funds) to amplify returns from an investment or project.

Like: a signal of approval or agreement, via clickable icon on a social media app.

Link: Highlighted text that sends the user to another online location when clicked on.

**Malicious Content**: Programs designed to disable, damage or steal data.

**Marketing Campaigns**: To promote products through different types of media, such as television, radio, print, and online platforms.

**Policy**: Is a principle of action adopted or proposed by a government, party, business, or individual.

**Principle**: Is a fundamental truth or proposition that serves as the foundation for a system of belief or behavior or for a chain of reasoning.

**Profile**: A user's personal area or page on social media app where the post content.

**Retail**: Is the sale of a product or service to an individual consumer for personal use.

**Share**: Forward, or re-post on social media.

Subscriber (or Follower): Someone who chooses to receive automatic updates from a particular social media account.

Target: In marketing, a target market is a group of potential customers to aims to reach with its products or services. This group may share common characteristics such as age, gender, income level, education, interests, and geographic location.

# BIBLIOGRAPHY

AIContentfy. (2023, August 11). The Art of Storytelling in Content Creation. Retrieved from AIContentfy: https://aicontentfy.com/en/blog/art-of-storytelling-in-content-creation#: :-text=It%20should%20have%20a%20clear,audience%20engaged%20throughout%20the%20story.

Alyssa Hirose, A. F. (2022, January 13). How to Promote Your YouTube Channel: 30 Tactics That Work. Retrieved from Hootsuite: https://blog.hootsuite.com/how-to-promote-your-youtube-channel/

Anderson, J. J. (2019). Should Kids Use Social Media? Chicago, Illinois: Norwood House Press.

Bathie, H. (2022). Social Media Survival Guide . Usborne.

Begg, R. (2019, November 07). How to Design a Logo [Step-by-Step Guide]. Retrieved from blog hubspot: https://blog.hubspot.com/marketing/how-to-design-logo

Contributors, W. (2023, September 11). Website. Retrieved from Wikipedia: https://en.wikipedia.org/wiki/Web_page#

D'souza, D. (2023, August 14). Investopedia. Retrieved from TikTok: What It Is, How It Works, and Why It's Popular: https://www.investopedia.com/what-is-tiktok-4588933

Entrepreneur, M. S. (2021). Entrepreneur Kids All about Social Media. Entrepreneur Press.

Hostinger. (2023, August 23). What Is HTML? . Retrieved from Hostinger Tutorials: https://www.hostinger.com/tutorials/what-is-html

JavaTpoint. (n.d.). What is a Webpage. Retrieved from Java T point: https://

www.javatpoint.com/what-is-a-web-page#: :text=It%20is%20very%20simple%20to,%2C%20the%20home%20page%2C%20etc.

Smith, A. N. (2023, August 11). Create Your Website in 9 Steps. Retrieved from digital.com: https://digital.com/how-to-create-a-website/

StopBullying.gov. (2021, November 10). Prevent Cyberbullying. Retrieved from StopBullying.gov: https://www.stopbullying.gov/cyberbullying/prevention

Wikipedia, C. (2002, May 22). Logo. Retrieved from Wikipedia: https://en.wikipedia.org/wiki/Logo

Wikipedia, C. (2023, September 19). Trademark. Retrieved from Wikipedia: https://en.wikipedia.org/w/index.php?title=Trademark&oldid=1176088681

Made in the USA
Monee, IL
18 October 2026

66036447R00090